SPANISH
à la Cartoon

Edited by
Albert H. Small, Ph.D.

with the assistance of
Lillian Tagle

PASSPORT BOOKS
NTC/Contemporary Publishing Group

Dedicated to
Jeff
Whose Grades in Spanish
Could Have Been Improved
by This Book

And With Special Thanks to
Bert Ludy and Nan Ronsheim

Published by Passport Books, a division of NTC Publishing Group.
© 1990 by NTC Publishing Group, 4255 West Touhy Avenue,
Lincolnwood (Chicago), Illinois 60646-1975 U.S.A.
All rights reserved. No part of this book may be reproduced, stored
in a retrieval system, or transmitted in any form or by any means,
electronic, mechanical, photocopying, recording or otherwise, without
the prior permission of NTC Publishing Group.
Manufactured in the United States of America.

11 12 13 14 VRS/VRS 0 4 3

Contents

A—Careful!—Word in Advance

When the ships of the Spanish Empire reached the shores of the New World almost five centuries ago, they brought with them a religion, a culture—and a language. Today the Spanish Empire is no more but with the exception of Brazil and some of the countries around the Caribbean, speakers of the language can be found from the banks of the Rio Grande to the plains of Patagonia, at the tip of South America.

More than that, Spanish is almost a second language in major parts of the United States. Many Americans are descendants of those who lived under Spanish rule in what are now the Southwestern and Western states. But they are doubtlessly outnumbered by the waves of Spanish-speaking peoples who have swept in from Puerto Rico, from Mexico and from other countries south of the border.

Indeed, *Time* magazine refers to "Spanglish" as an intermediate language where American Spanish and English meet, as in *¿Dónde está el vacuum cleaner?* ("Where is the vacuum cleaner?") and "Do you have any *cerveza?*" (beer). For some people the mixture of Spanish and English has become so complete that a Spanish-speaking youngster is reported to have asked his mother "How do you say *ice cream* in English?" And Spanish verbs (pronounced as in Spanish) have even been made from English words: like *monkear,* to monkey around; *shopear,* to go shopping; and *mopear,* to mop the floor.

But beware the differences between Spanish and English! Words in Spanish that may seem the same as in English can have sharply different meanings. A *Boletín de Denuncia* may be not a denunciation, but a traffic ticket. And an American lady, visiting a Spanish-speaking country, who says she is embarrassed (*me siento embarazada*) can REALLY be embarrassed—because she has announced instead that she is pregnant!

Embarrassment is bad enough, but an American businessman can lose a lot of money by using the wrong word. In a negotiation with a Spanish-speaking businessman, the American might want to compromise on price or terms— for example to "split the difference" between what he is offering and what the Spanish-speaking businessman seems willing to accept. But if he uses the word *compromiso,* he is making a commitment instead! He needs to use the verb *transigir* or *transar*.

Spanish-speaking people often "have" (*tener*) what English-speaking people "are." A Spanish-speaking child will say proudly "I *have* five years" (*Tengo cinco años*). And, in Spanish, you have thirst (*tiene sed*) and have hunger (*tiene hambre*) rather than being thirsty or hungry.

Then too, subject pronouns may be reserved for extreme emphasis. You may say in Spanish "Am happy" (*Estoy contento*) rather than "I am happy"; and "Is coming" (*Viene*) rather than "he is coming."

Spanish sometimes offers shades of meaning not available in English. When the annoyed wife, visiting the marriage counselor, wants to get the attention of her spouse, she can say in English "He's talking to YOU, stupid!" But in Spanish she can say *¡A ti te están hablando, estúpido!* (literally: "You, he's talking to you, stupid!"), thus providing emphasis in the written as well as the spoken language.

Remember we mentioned the spread of Spanish from the Rio Grande to the tip of South America. But the Spanish spoken in the sixteen Latin American countries and Spain is not completely the same. Identical words or expressions can mean different things in different Spanish-speaking countries.

Guagua means "baby" in Chile and Colombia. In Cuba and some Caribbean and Central American countries it means "bus." A pregnant woman from Chile, meeting a friend from Guatemala on the street, announced that she was expecting a baby. The surprised answer was "But this is not a bus stop!"

Then there is the story of the British ambassador, accredited to a Latin American country, who asked a mischievous colleague what words to use when being presented to the President and his cabinet. The colleague suggested words and phrases in Spanish that sounded quite ordinary and appropriate. Unfortunately, in that country, some of the words had a very improper connotation. The presentation was a disaster—the President and his cabinet burst into irrepressible laughter in the midst of the ceremony. Moral: ask somebody you can trust when the Spanish words you use are going to be important!

The cartoons in this book were chosen because the humor can be translated into English from Spanish. For example, you can say in Spanish *or* in English that a nasty fellow is a "pig," and one of our cartoonists illustrates the point.

But note well: the literal translation and the "Everyday English" caption at the bottom of the page can be quite different. In effect, what we have sometimes done is to re-caption the cartoon as an American editor might in adapting a Spanish cartoon for an American newspaper or magazine. This not only improves the joke, but often sharply illustrates the difference between Spanish and English conversational idioms. And that's the purpose of the book. To help take you away from the routine rules of syntax and vocabulary, and bring you out to the world of people speaking Spanish in ordinary circumstances. In addition, to make the pages easier to read, we have usually repeated the artist's lettering in the caption under the cartoon.

Why choose humor as a learning aid? Obviously because humor is an enjoyable way for getting anything done. But more than that: the key to learning is *memory*—and for almost everybody there is nothing more memorable than a really good joke.

So please don't blame us if you remember the Spanish word for "spots" by identifying it with a cartoon of a cow at the cosmetics counter. Or associate the word for "sickness" with a doctor in a glass case. Or if the Spanish phrase for a speeding ticket suggests an angry mother-in-law in the living room. Not to mention the Spanish for "stolen car" reminding you of the daughter who has eloped.

Good reading—and good laughing!

A Technical Comment—or Two

Learning a language can be fun, especially when it helps you understand the punch line of a joke or the conversation at a get-together. But let's face it—learning a language can also get complicated. In this book we're going to try to keep as much of the fun as we can, and burden you with a minimum of complications.

Basically, the vocabulary provided in this book is an aid to understanding the cartoons. We won't give you *all* the possible translations of a Spanish word—just the ones that relate to the material at hand.

And we won't bother translating the words you can figure out for yourself—even in cases where the spelling differs somewhat from the spelling in English. But please be alert for the different ways in which such words can be used in Spanish. *Fútbol* in Spanish, for example, refers to soccer rather than the American game of football; a *librería* is a bookstore rather than a library. And even Spanish words that have become popular in the United States may have a meaning different from their English-language sound-alikes. For example, *simpático* doesn't mean sympathetic, but rather agreeable or congenial.

Incidentally, we've used some fairly obvious abbreviations: *n.* for noun, *adj.* for adjective, *adv.* for adverb, *v.* for verb, *inf.* for infinitive, *conj.* for conjunction, *m.* for masculine, *f.* for feminine. To help you recognize a verb in other usages, we add the infinitive form (when the infinitive isn't used in the cartoon caption) along with the verb form that is used.

To avoid cluttering up the vocabulary list under each cartoon, we've given you three sections to handle the most common words. **Pronouns** are an especially important part of everyday speech, so you will want to be familiar with all the common ones. Then, the **Five Important Verbs**—Spanish for "to be," "to have," and "to go"—are important for themselves and as helper verbs, just as in English. You will want to recognize all their forms on sight. Finally, **The Little Words** are the ones that link together ordinary speech—words like *the, but, here, because* and so forth. Rather than listing these words every time they appear in a cartoon caption, we've brought them together in this list to encourage you to make sure they are a basic part of your Spanish vocabulary.

The Pronouns

This is not an exhaustive list of pronouns in Spanish. Rather, it is an illustration of how common pronouns you will encounter in the cartoon captions can be used in conversation.

Subject Pronouns

Yo hablo.	**I** talk.
Tú hablas.	**You** (sing., familiar) talk.
Usted habla.	**You** (sing., formal) talk.
Él habla.	**He** talks.
Ella habla.	**She** talks.
Nosotros hablamos.	**We** (m.) talk.
Nosotras hablamos.	**We** (f.) talk.
Ustedes hablan.	**You** (pl., formal) talk.
Ellos hablan.	**They** (m., pl.) talk.
Ellas hablan.	**They** (f, pl.) talk.

Direct Object Pronouns

Ella **me** ve.	She sees **me.**
Ella **te** ve.	She sees **you** (sing., familiar).
Yo **lo** veo.	I see **him.**
Yo **la** veo.	I see **her.**
Ella **nos** ve.	She sees **us.**
Yo **los** veo.	I see **you/them** (m., pl.).
Yo **las** veo.	I see **you/them** (f., pl.).

Indirect Object Pronouns

El **me** da el lápiz.	He gives **me** the pencil.
El **te** da el lápiz.	He gives **you** (sing., familiar) the pencil.
Yo **le** doy el lápiz.	I give **him/her/you** (sing., formal) the pencil.
El **nos** da el lápiz.	He gives **us** the pencil.
Yo **les** doy el lápiz.	I give **them/you** (pl., formal) the pencil.

Double Object Pronouns

Yo **se lo** doy.	I am giving **it** to **him/her/them.**
Ellos **te lo** dan.	They (m.) are giving **it** to **you.**
Nosotros **se lo** damos.	We are giving **it** to **him/her/them.**
Ella **nos lo** da.	She is giving **it** to **us.**
Ustedes **se la** dan.	You are giving **it** to **him/her/them.**

Demonstrative and Possessive Pronouns

Ese es **el mío.**	**That**'s **mine** (subject is masculine).
Esa es **la mía.**	**That**'s **mine** (subject is feminine).
Este es **el suyo.**	**This** is **his/hers/theirs.**
Ese es **el nuestro.**	**That**'s **ours.**
Ese es **el suyo.**	**That**'s **yours.**
Esta de acá es **la suya.**	**This one** is **theirs** (subject feminine).

Two Relative Pronouns

La gente **que** viene.	People **who** come.
¿Quién es?	**Who** is it?

Reflexive Pronouns

Yo **me** llamo Juan.	I'm named John. (I call **myself** Juan.)
El **se** llama Juan.	He's named John. (He calls **himself** Juan.)

NOTE: In Spanish the pronouns may be attached to the verbs when used in commands. For example *Dáselo* ("Give it to him") is a combination of the verb *dar*, the indirect object *se*, and the direct object *lo*.

REMINDER! In spoken and written Spanish the subject pronoun may be omitted. Example: *Estoy contento* ("I am happy").

Five Important Verbs

	to be	to be	to have	to have	to go
	ser	**estar**	**haber**	**tener**	**ir**
Present					
	yo soy	yo estoy	yo he	yo tengo	yo voy
	tú eres	tú estás	tú has	tú tienes	tú vas
	él es	él está	él ha	él tiene	él va
	nosotros somos	nosotros estamos	nosotros hemos	nosotros tenemos	nosotros vamos
	vosotros sois	vosotros estáis	vosotros habéis	vosotros tenéis	vosotros vais
	ustedes son	ustedes están	ustedes han	ustedes tienen	ustedes van
	ellos son	ellos están	ellos han	ellos tienen	ellos van
Future					
	yo seré	yo estaré	yo habré	yo tendré	yo iré
	tú serás	tú estarás	tú habrás	tú tendrás	tú irás
	él será	él estará	él habrá	él tendrá	él irá
	nosotros seremos	nosotros estaremos	nosotros habremos	nosotros tendremos	nosotros iremos
	vosotros seréis	vosotros estaréis	vosotros habréis	vosotros tendréis	vosotros iréis
	ustedes serán	ustedes estarán	ustedes habrán	ustedes tendrán	ustedes irán
	ellos serán	ellos estarán	ellos habrán	ellos tendrán	ellos irán

Five Important Verbs

	to be		to have		to go
	ser	**estar**	**haber**	**tener**	**ir**

Past (Preterite)

ser	**estar**	**haber**	**tener**	**ir**
yo fui	yo estuve	yo hube	yo tuve	yo fui
tú fuiste	tú estuviste	tú hubiste	tú tuviste	tú fuiste
él fue	él estuvo	él hubo	él tuvo	él fue
nosotros fuimos	nosotros estuvimos	nosotros hubimos	nosotros tuvimos	nosotros fuimos
vosotros fuisteis	vosotros estuvisteis	vosotros hubisteis	vosotros tuvisteis	vosotros fuisteis
ustedes fueron	ustedes estuvieron	ustedes hubieron	ustedes tuvieron	ustedes fueron
ellos fueron	ellos estuvieron	ellos hubieron	ellos tuvieron	ellos fueron

Note: To save space, we have used only the masculine forms of pronouns in this chart. For the feminine forms, see *The Pronouns*. Also, remember that the *vosotros* form is only used in Spain. In Latin America, *ustedes* is used as "you" plural.

The Little Words

A refresher on some of the common words that hold the conversation together.

a, al	to, at, for, to the
ahora	now
antes	before
aquí	here
como	like
con	with
de, del	of, from, of the
desde	since
el	the (m.)
en	in
entonces	then
hoy	today
la, las, los	the
más	more

ni	neither ... nor
no	not, no
nunca	never
o	or
para	to, for
pero	but
por	of, from
por favor	please
porque	because
¿por qué?	why?
sí	yes
si	if
siempre	always
sin	without
también	also
tan	so
tanto	so much, as much
todavía	still
un, una, uno	one
y	and

Introducing . . . the Artists!

Leonardo Aguaslimpias Feldrich (AGUASLIMPIAS)—from Colombia—is not only a self-taught artist, but has also had a career as a boxer (12 bouts, with only one loss), and is by avocation a poet.

Even as a twelve-year-old he wanted to study art, but family finances made that impossible. Eventually, two of his teachers helped, and he was able to earn a school diploma and to study for one semester at the School of Architecture of the University of Atlantico.

Though never having the benefit of formal studies, his drawings are said to reflect the worries and passions of the common people. From boxing he feels he learned the discipline necessary for his artistic efforts. He has explored surrealism, with human figures having objects in place of their heads. Happily, the drawings in this book are more conventional!

Aguaslimpias has participated in group exhibitions in 1983 and 1984, and has had one-man shows—one in 1982 and three in 1987.

Cesar Augusto Almeida Remolina (KEKAR)—also from Colombia—was born in 1956 in Rionegro, in Santander Province. He began his professional career in 1974 with the newspaper *Vanguardia Liberal* of Bucaramanga.

His collaborations include the newspaper *El Tiempo* of Bogotá; the weekly *Nueva Frontera;* the newspaper *El Mundo* of Medellín; the magazine *Diners y Cromos;* and the publication "Education and Culture" of the Colombian Federation of Educators.

His works have been exhibited at the Industrial University in Santander; the Museum of Contemporary Art, at the Colombo-American Center; and the Santa Fe Gallery in Bogotá.

He published a book in 1984, *Speaking of Social, Political and Other Matters*. In 1983 he won the Simón Bolívar prize for his works in the newspaper *Vanguardia Liberal,* for which he still works.

Victor M. Cartin Brenes (TIN-GLAO)—from Costa Rica—was born in San José 29 years ago, where he had his primary and secondary education. He then studied industrial design for the shoe industry at the School of Clothing Art of the University of Perugia, Italy. Returning to San José, he received a degree in industrial relations at the Colegio Latinum UACA there.

He is the author of *An Anthology of Humor*, published in 1982 by the Ministry of Sports, Youth, and Culture. His work appears in a number of magazines, including *Rumbo Centramericano* and *Perfil*, and in *La Nación*, the morning newspaper with the country's largest circulation.

His honors include awards from the Humor Biennial in Havana in 1983; and participation in an exhibit of political satire in Mexico.

He has taken a special interest in rural health, and prepared publications on that subject in Costa Rica in 1984. He also prepared illustrations for a book on the Aqueducts of Latin America, published by the Pan American Health Organization.

Percy Eaglehurst (PERCY)—from Chile—was born in Antofagasta where he received his primary and secondary education.

He continued his education in Santiago at the University of Chile, where he studied fine arts at the Construction School of the Institute of Physical Education and, later, at the Institute for Technical Education. He has a degree as Professor of Advertising Art.

After teaching at various colleges, he became Vice Chancellor for Communication at the University of Chile, and Director of the university's magazine.

From his student days he has been contributing to newspapers and magazines in the capital and in the provinces. In his 42 years as a cartoonist he has received many honors, including an opportunity to come to the United States to attend the Walt Disney Study Center.

Arcadio Esquivel (ARCADIO)—from Costa Rica—was born in 1959 at Alajuela. At the age of 20 he obtained a degree in civil construction and technical drawing from the College of Industrial Technology of Calle Blancos. He also studied cartooning and graphic humor at the CEAC School, from which he received a certificate in 1982; he studied advertising art and painting at the University of Costa Rica.

His first exhibition, in 1981, was a collection of comic art entitled *La Pluma Sonriente* (the Smiling Pen). Since then his work has been exhibited in Germany, Cuba, Japan, Panama, and Puerto Rico.

He received prizes in 1981 and in 1985, both in Costa Rica and in Puerto Rico. His work has appeared in a series of periodicals in Costa Rica as well as in Nicaragua and in *El Noticiero SIP* in Miami.

Omar Alberto Figueroa Turcios (OFIT)—from Colombia— was born 20 years ago in Corozal, in the province of Sucre. He received his primary education there and his secondary education in Barranquilla.

In Barranquilla he studied advertising and advertising art. In 1985 he began contributing to *El Heraldo* and *Diario del Caribe*. He now writes a daily column, and one on Sunday called *Sacapuntas* (the pencil sharpener) in which he reviews events of the week.

The youngest of eight brothers, he is the only one who produces cartoon humor, although two other brothers are journalists with major Barranquilla newspapers.

Antonio Fraguas de Pablo (FORGES)—from Spain—was born in Madrid in 1942, the second of nine brothers. He became an electronic engineer in the technical department of Spanish television. But at the age of 21 he had his first cartoon published in a daily newspaper, and has been cartooning ever since. He finally left electronics, and became so popular in Spain that there is literally a "Forges style."

His newspaper cartoons have appeared in *Diario 16* (daily), *Correo del Norte*, *Diario Vasco*, and *Reus Diari*. News magazines, including *Interviu*, *El Jueves* and *Diez Minutos* have also published his cartoons.

In addition to regularly published cartoons, Forges has illustrated the text of various types of books, including some on golf, medicine, and electronics.

He is married and has four children—three girls and a boy—and spends his leisure time playing golf and enjoying music and literature.

Luis Asenjo (OSSES)—from Chile—brings daily life in Chile to his drawings, yet with a sly humor.

In the cities, the drivers are trying to outmaneuver the traffic cops, just as in the United States. The drunk confides in the bartender, and the picnickers discover the trash where they left it last year.

But in the countryside a couple is trying to make the best of it during one of Chile's floods; the farm woman is coping with her first baby in the only way she knows how; and the hunter is trying to reason with his dog after accidentally shooting him in the tail.

The characters of **Pablo San José (PABLO)**—from Spain— became familiar to the public in that country through their weekly appearances: the sinister characters of the office, the lady with Victorian ideals, the school girls in their uniforms, their teachers, the gypsy with the tame bear. His cartoons have also appeared "in the five continents and their adjacent islands."

Born in Larache, North Africa, when that city was part of Spanish Morocco, Pablo is also well known for his illustrated lectures on the history of graphic humor in Spain. Given in Spanish, and rapidly illustrated by the speaker during the talk, the lectures have proven popular enough to travel from Spain to Holland. Some day they may be delighting advanced students of Spanish here in the United States.

Luis Sayán Puente (SAYÁN)—from Peru: South America has its own version of Superman, and in Peru the character has been brought to life as *Hatun-Kuntur,* literally Super Cóndor, using words from the ancient Inca language.

Sayán has illustrated the exploits of this mythical bird in a fast-moving picture-story entitled *The Kidnapping of Michael Jackson.*

But Sr. Sayán, as can be seen from the pages of this book, is also capable of picturing a relaxed humor based on the problems of daily life.

Oscar Sierra (OKI) is a 34-year-old Colombian who has lived in Costa Rica since 1979, and has been busy translating the myths and legends of Central America into comic strips in order to preserve them for youngsters growing up in today's "audiovisual age."

Along with two of his brothers ("we were born with brushes in our hands" he says), he has researched the lore of Latin America. "Our continent has the world's eyes upon it now, mostly because of its political and social problems," he says. "That's the negative part, the poor, sad side. What hasn't been shown yet is the cultural wealth of Latin America—the poetic concept, the vision of the universe, that these cultures have."

His cartoons on these pages are myths of a more universal nature.

Rafael Ruiz Tejada B. (Ruizte)—from Mexico—was born just before Christmas, 548 months ago in Atzcapotzalco "next to the oil refinery." He studied drawing, painting, sculpture, and engraving at the National School of Plastic Arts in San Carlos. Since 1958 he has been producing animated cartoons. In his free time he paints and experiments with new techniques for animated films.

As a member of the Mexican Cartoonists Society, his works have appeared in Germany, Belgium, Bulgaria, Canada, Cuba, Italy, and Nicaragua. Since 1963 his cartoons have appeared in various newspapers, including *El Universal, Ovaciones, Rotativo,* and *El Nacional.* They have also appeared in a variety of magazines, including *D'Etiqueta, Sucesos, Caso Clínico, La Capital, Contrapunto, Nueva Vida, Eros, Ser, Rayas,* and *Chispa.*

Some familiar characters regularly make their appearance in Ruizte's cartoons: the insignificant husband, the cranky wife, and the perpetual celebrant. Yet through it all humor sweeps away their cares.

Luis Elcíades Mosquera (Elcíades)—from Colombia—has been drawing cartoons for Colombia's newspapers for over 22 years. He studied cartooning at the Continental Academy of Bogotá and advertising art at El Sena School in Cali.

His cartoons have appeared in *El Expreso, El Occidente* and *El País* in Cali; *La Patria* in Manizales; *El Colombiano* in Medellín; *La República* and *El Espacio,* as well as the magazine *Cromos,* in Bogotá.

Awards have been given to his cartoons in exhibitions in New York, Montreal, Grabovo (Bulgaria), Athens, Tolentino (Italy), Piracicaba (Brazil) and Berlin.

SPANISH
à la Cartoon

Aguaslimpias (Colombia)

—¿Cómo que sin fondos? Si todavía tengo 5 cheques en la chequera.

Key Words

fondos (*n., m.*)	funds
todavía (*adv.*)	still
chequera (*n., f.*)	checkbook

Everyday English

"What do you mean I'm broke? I still have five checks in my checkbook!"

Aguaslimpias (Colombia)

—¿Que no estás borracho? Sigue esta línea recta si es que puedes.

Key Words

borracho (*adj.*)	drunk
sigue (*v.*, seguir *inf.*)	follow
línea (*n.*, *f.*)	line
recta (*adj.*)	straight
puedes (*v.*, poder *inf.*)	can

Everyday English

"You're not drunk? Follow this straight line if you can."

Aguaslimpias (Colombia)

—¡Embuste! Hoy no hubo pelea . . . vi la televisión. El ojo te lo hizo el marido de la vecina del segundo piso.

Key Words

embuste (*n., m.*)	lie, falsehood
hubo (*v.*, haber *inf.*)	there was
pelea (*n., f.*)	fight
vi (*v.*, ver *inf.*)	watched, was watching
ojo (*n., m.*)	eye (here, black eye)
marido (*n., m.*)	husband
vecina (*n., f.*)	neighbor
segundo piso (*n., m.*)	second floor

Everyday English

"Liar! There was no fight today . . . I was watching television. You got that black eye from our neighbor's husband on the second floor."

Aguaslimpias (Colombia)

—Es el arma más terrible. Ojalá el hombre no la utilice jamás.
Acabaría con la raza humana . . .

Key Words

arma (*n., f.*)	weapon
ojalá (*exclam.*)	let's hope
hombre (*n., m.*)	man
utilice (*v.*, utilizar *inf.*)	use
jamás (*adv.*)	never
acabaría (*v.*, acabar *inf.*)	would end
raza humana (*n., f.*)	human race

Everyday English

"It's a terrible weapon. Let's hope man never uses it; it would
be the end of the human race."

Kekar (Colombia)

—Así es, señor . . . en ese libro escribí mis memorias y en este otro todo lo que se me olvidó . . .

Key Words

así es	that's it
libro (*n., m.*)	book
escribí (*v.,* escribir *inf.*)	wrote
memorias (*n., f.*)	memoirs
otro (*adj.*)	other
olvidó (*v.,* olvidar *inf.*)	forgot

Everyday English

"Yes, sir. In that book I wrote my memoirs and in this one, everything I forgot."

—¡Terribles noticias, querido . . . ! ¡Ejecutaron a nuestro hijo en la cacerola eléctrica!

Key Words

noticias (*n., f.*)	news
querido (*n., m.*)	dear
hijo (*n., m.*)	son
cacerola (*n., f.*)	frying pan

Everyday English

"Dreadful news, my dear! Our son has been executed in the electric frying pan!"

Kekar (Colombia)

—Usted es autónomo en su decisión, señor Presidente . . . ¿Qué dice: se va o lo echamos . . . ?

Key Words

dice (*v.*, decir *inf.*)	say
se va (*v.*, irse *inf.*)	you leave
echamos (*v.*, echar *inf.*)	we oust

Everyday English

"You're free to decide Mr. President. . . What do you say: will you leave or do we oust you?"

Tin-Glao (Costa Rica)

—Mi amor . . . ¿Qué estás pensando?
—Lo mismo que vos, mi palomita.
—¡Cerdo!

Key Words

mi amor	my love
pensando (*v.*, pensar *inf.*)	thinking
(lo) mismo	same (thing)
palomita (*n.*, *f.*)	little dove
cerdo (*n.*, *m.*)	pig

Everyday English

"My love, what are you thinking?"
"The same thing you are, my little dove."
"Pig!"

Tin-Glao (Costa Rica)

—¿Le traigo una boquita de chicharrón?

Key Words

traigo (*v.*, traer *inf.*)	bring
boquita (*n.*, *f.*)	bite, hors d'oeuvre
chicharrón (*n.*, *m.*)	pork rind

Everyday English

"May I bring you a bite of pork rinds?"

Tin-Glao (Costa Rica)

—¿Quién le dijo que todavía usábamos bola de cristal?

Key Words

dijo (*v.*, decir *inf.*)	said, told
usábamos (*v.*, usar *inf.*)	used
bola de cristal (*n.*, *f.*)	crystal ball

Everyday English

"Who told you we still use a crystal ball?"

Tin-Glao (Costa Rica)

—Mamá . . . ¿De verdad soy venenoso?

Key Words

| de verdad | truly, really |
| venenoso (*adj.*) | poisonous |

Everyday English

"Mama, am I really poisonous?"

—Piensa que soy su mamá . . .

Key Words

piensa (*v.*, pensar *inf.*)   thinks

Everyday English

"He thinks I'm his mother . . ."

Tin-Glao (Costa Rica)

—¿Tiene alguna crema para borrar manchas?

Key Words

tiene (*v.*, tener *inf.*)	have
alguna (*adj.*)	any
crema (*n.*, *f.*)	cream
borrar (*v.*, *inf.*)	erase
manchas (*n.*, *f.*)	spots

Everyday English

"Do you have a cream to cover spots?"

Tin-Glao (Costa Rica)

—Me preocupa la vejez . . .

—Despreocúpate . . .
¡Que al final de tu
vida el dinero te
lloverá del cielo!

Key Words

preocupa (*v.*, preocupar *inf.*)	worry
vejez (*n., f.*)	old age
final (*n., m.*)	end
vida (*n., f.*)	life
dinero (*n., m.*)	money
lloverá (*v.*, llover *inf.*)	will rain, will shower
cielo (*n., m.*)	heaven

Everyday English

"I'm worried about my old age."
"Stop worrying. At the end of your life you'll be showered with money from heaven!"

Tin-Glao (Costa Rica)

—Mi amor . . . prométeme que nunca más volverás a ordenar en francés . . .

Key Words

mi amor	my love
prométeme (*v.*, prometer *inf.*)	promise me
nunca (*adv.*)	never
volverás a (*v.*, volver *inf.*)	will do again
ordenar (*v.*, *inf.*)	order
francés (*n.*, *m.*)	French

Everyday English

"My love, promise me you'll never again order in French..."

Tin-Glao (Costa Rica)

—No, no hijito . . . Si vivimos en la capital . . . somos capitalinos . . . no capitalistas . . . ¿Ehh?

Key Words

hijo, hijito (*n., m.*)   son, little son
vivimos (*v.,* vivir *inf.*)   we live
capitalinos (*n., m.*)   inhabitants of the capital
    city

Everyday English

"No, my son, the fact that we live in the capital doesn't make us capitalists."

Tin-Glao (Costa Rica)

—Abuelita . . . Se me hace un nudo en la garganta cada vez que te veo tirada en ese rincón.

Key Words

abuelita (*n., f.*)	grandmother (diminutive)
nudo (*n., m.*)	knot
garganta (*n., f.*)	throat
cada vez que (*conj.*)	whenever
veo (*v.*, ver *inf.*)	see
tirada (*v.*, tirar *inf.*)	thrown away
rincón (*n., m.*)	corner

Everyday English

"Grandma, I get a lump in my throat every time I see you thrown away in that corner."

Tin-Glao (Costa Rica)

—No, mi amor . . . Aquí en la oficina . . . nadie ha notado que me puse peluquín . . .

Key Words

mi amor	my love
oficina (*n., f.*)	office
nadie (*pronoun*)	nobody
ha notado (*v., notar inf.*)	has noticed
puse (*v., ponerse inf.*)	put on, wear
peluquín (*n., m.*)	hairpiece, toupee

Everyday English

"No, my love . . . Here in the office nobody noticed that I'm wearing a toupee."

Tin-Glao (Costa Rica)

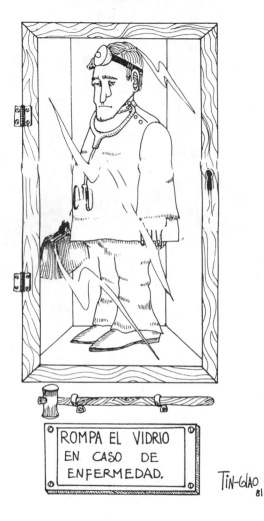

ROMPA EL VIDRIO
EN CASO DE
ENFERMEDAD.

Tin-Glao 81

Key Words

rompa (*v.,* romper *inf.*)	break
vidrio (*n., m.*)	glass
en caso de (*prep.*)	in case of
enfermedad (*n., f.*)	illness

Everyday English

Break glass in case of illness.

Tin-Glao (Costa Rica)

—. . . Pues yo siempre creí que ustedes eran cosa de cuentos . . .
—¡Qué casualidad! Yo también . . .

Key Words

creí (*v.*, creer *inf.*)	believed
cosa (*n.*, *f.*)	thing
cuentos (*n.*, *m.*)	stories, fiction
casualidad (*n.*, *f.*)	chance, coincidence

Everyday English

"I always thought you were just make-believe."
"What a coincidence! That's what I thought you were."

Tin-Glao (Costa Rica)

—Señor, ayúdame a decidir . . . ¿Pinto la rubia o la morena?

Key Words

ayúdame (*v.*, ayudar *inf.*)	help me
decidir (*v.*, *inf.*)	decide
pinto (*v.*, pintar *inf.*)	paint
rubia (*n.*, *f.*)	blonde
morena (*n.*, *f.*)	brunette

Everyday English

"Lord, help me decide. Do I paint the blonde or the brunette?"

Tin-Glao (Costa Rica)

Key Words

especialista (*n., m.* or *f.*)	specialist
garganta (*n., f.*)	throat
oídos (*n., m.*)	ears
nariz (*n., f.*)	nose

Everyday English

Dr. Pérez, ear, nose and throat specialist.

Tin-Glao (Costa Rica)

—¡Pobre Carmen! . . . Desde que padece de vértigo, ya no es la misma . . .

Key Words

pobre (*adj.*)	poor
padece (*v.*, padecer *inf.*)	suffer
misma (*adj.*)	same

Everyday English

"Poor Carmen, she's not the same since that attack of vertigo."

Percy (Chile)

—Avísale tú, que está despedido.

Key Words

avísale (*v.*, avisar *inf.*)	tell him
despedido	fired

Everyday English

"*You* tell him he's fired."

Percy (Chile)

—Habla de un plan para asegurar la paz en forma permanente.

Key Words

habla (*v.*, hablar *inf.*)	speaks
plan (*n.*, *m.*)	plan
asegurar (*v.*, *inf.*)	to insure
paz (*n.*, *f.*)	peace

Everyday English

"It speaks here about a plan to insure permanent peace."

Percy (Chile)

—Señor, somos de la Liga Protectora de la Mujer.

Key Words

somos (*v.*, ser *inf.*)	we are
liga (*n.*, *f.*)	league
mujer (*n.*, *f.*)	woman

Everyday English

"Sir, we are from the League for the Protection of Women."

Percy (Chile)

—Un helado para ellos y tres cervezas para mí.

Key Words

helado (*n., m.*)	ice cream
tres	three
cervezas (*n., f.*)	beers

Everyday English

"One ice cream for them and three beers for me."

Percy (Chile)

—Pregunta si nos vamos a quedar mucho tiempo . . .

Key Words

pregunta (*v.*, preguntar *inf.*)	he asks
vamos (*v.*, ir *inf.*)	we are going
quedarnos (*v.*, quedarse *inf.*)	to stay
mucho tiempo	long time

Everyday English

"He wants to know if we're going to stay long."

Percy (Chile)

—¿Vas a bajar a almorzar?
—¿Estás loco? ¿No has visto lo peligroso que está el tránsito?

Key Words

bajar (*v., inf.*)	go down
almorzar (*v., inf.*)	to have lunch
loco (*adj.*)	crazy
visto (*v.,* ver *inf.*)	seen
peligroso (*adj.*)	dangerous
tránsito (*n., m.*)	traffic

Everyday English

"Going down for lunch?"
"Are you crazy? Can't you see how dangerous the traffic is?"

Percy (Chile)

—Señora . . . ¿No ha intentado usar la psicología con su hijo?

Key Words

intentado (*v.*, intentar *inf.*)	tried
usar (*v.*, *inf.*)	to use
psicología (*n.*, *f.*)	psychology
hijo (*n.*, *m.*)	son

Everyday English

"Madam, have you tried using psychology on your son?"

Percy (Chile)

—Es carísimo el equipo, de modo que lo financio con algunos consejos comerciales . . .

Key Words

carísimo (*adj.*)	very expensive
financio (*v.*, financiar *inf.*)	finance
algunos (*adj.*)	some
consejos comerciales (*n., m.*)	advertisements, commercials

Everyday English

"The equipment is so expensive I try to defray the cost by showing commercials."

—¡A ti te están hablando, estúpido!

Key Words

consejero matrimonial (*n., m.*)	marriage counselor
hablando (*v.,* hablar *inf.*)	talking
estúpido (*n., m.*)	stupid person

Everyday English

"He's talking to YOU, stupid!"
(Sign says: Marriage Counselor
   • Psychologist
   • Professor
   • Marriage Specialist)

Percy (Chile)

—Difícil solucionarle sus peticiones pero con este sistema por lo menos le calmamos los nervios.

Key Words

sugerencias (*n., f.*)	suggestions
quejas (*n., f.*)	complaints
difícil (*adj.*)	difficult
solucionarle (*v., inf.*)	to solve (for him)
peticiones (*n., f.*)	requests
sistema (*n., m.*)	system
por lo menos	at least
calmamos (*v.,* calmar *inf.*)	we soothe
nervios (*n., m.*)	nerves

Everyday English

"It's hard to do anything about his requests, but at least this system calms his nerves."

Percy (Chile)

—... ¡y como sólo dejo deudas, mis herederos deberán repartírselas sin pelear!

Key Words

sólo (*adv.*)	only
dejo (*v.*, dejar *inf.*)	leave
deudas (*n.*, *f.*)	debts
herederos (*n.*, *m.*)	heirs
deberán (*v.*, deber *inf.*)	will have to
repartírselas (*v.*, repartir *inf.*)	share them
pelear (*v.*, *inf.*)	quarrel

Everyday English

"... and since I leave only debts, my heirs will have to divide them up without quarreling over them."

Percy (Chile)

—Comprendo que tengas temor a los terremotos y te acuestes vestido, pero creo que exageras.

Key Words

comprendo (*v.*, comprender *inf.*)	understand
temor (*n.*, *m.*)	fear
terremotos (*n.*, *m.*)	earthquakes
acuestes (*v.*, acostarse *inf.*)	go to bed
vestido (*v.*, vestir *inf.*)	dressed
creo (*v.*, creer *inf.*)	believe

Everyday English

"I know you're afraid of earthquakes, but I think going to bed dressed is overdoing it."

Percy (Chile)

—¡Mira Juan, éste es el hombre que abolió la esclavitud!

Key Words

mira (*v.*, mirar *inf.*)	look
hombre (*n.*, *m.*)	man
abolió (*v.*, abolir *inf.*)	abolish
esclavitud (*n.*, *f.*)	slavery

Everyday English

"Look, Juan, there's the man who abolished slavery."

Percy (Chile)

—¿Es astronauta su marido?
—No. Es alérgico a los mosquitos . . .

Key Words

astronauta (*n., m.*)	astronaut
marido (*n., m.*)	husband
alérgico (*adj.*)	allergic

Everyday English

"Is your husband an astronaut?"
"No, he's allergic to mosquitoes."

Percy (Chile)

—Vieron entrar ahí a mi primo pero no ha salido.

Key Words

vieron (*v.*, ver *inf.*)	saw
entrar (*v.*, *inf.*)	enter
ahí (*adv.*)	there
primo (*n.*, *m.*)	cousin
salido (*v.*, salir *inf.*)	come out, leave

Everyday English

"They saw my cousin go in there, but he hasn't come out."

Percy (Chile)

—¡Perdón señor, no le puedo informar. Estoy recién ingresado a esta oficina.

Key Words

puedo (*v.*, poder *inf.*)	am able to
informar (*v.*, *inf.*)	inform
recién (*adv.*)	recently
ingresado (*v.*, ingresar *inf.*)	entered, became a member
oficina (*n.*, *f.*)	office

Everyday English

"I'm sorry sir, I'm not able to answer your question. I just got into this office."

Arcadio (Costa Rica)

—¡Disculpe, pero no me gusta venir en auto a la oficina!

Key Words

disculpe (*v.*, disculpar *inf.*)	excuse (me)
gusta (*v.*, gustar *inf.*)	like
venir (*v.*, *inf.*)	come
oficina (*n.*, *f.*)	office

Everyday English

"Excuse me, but I don't like to bring my car to the office."

40

Arcadio (Costa Rica)

—¿Ahora comprende lo de la almohada?

Key Words

comprende (*v.*, comprender *inf.*)	understand
almohada (*n.*, *f.*)	pillow

Everyday English

"Now do you understand the reason for the pillow?"

Arcadio (Costa Rica)

—Talvés no sea reglamentario . . . ¡Pero no me va a negar que es un marco encantador!

Key Words

talvés = tal vez (*adv.*)	perhaps
reglamentario (*adj.*)	pertaining to regulations
negar (*v., inf.*)	deny
marco (*n., m.*)	goal
encantador (*adj.*)	charming

Everyday English

"Perhaps it's not regulation, but you can't deny it's a charming goal!"

Arcadio (Costa Rica)

—¿Y qué? ¿Tiene algo de malo que el balón sea teledirigido?

Key Words

balón (*n., m.*)	(soccer) ball
algo de malo	anything wrong
teledirigido (*adj.*)	radio-controlled

Everyday English

"So what? What's wrong with a radio-controlled ball?"

Ofit (Colombia)

LA GENTE SE QUEJA QUE
EN LA T.V. SE PRESENTAN
PROGRAMAS QUE TRAS
DE SER EXTRANJEROS
SON VIOLENTOS...

...SERA QUE LA VIOLENCIA
CRIOLLA NO DA PARA
BUENOS PROGRAMAS?!

—La gente se queja que en la T.V. se presentan programas que tras de ser extranjeros son violentos. . . . Será que la violencia criolla no da para buenos programas?!

Key Words

gente (*n., f.*)	people
se queja (*v.*, quejarse *inf.*)	complain
tras de ser	besides being
extranjeros (*adj.*)	foreign
criolla (*adj.*)	local, national
buenos (*adj.*)	good

Everyday English

"People complain that TV programs are not only foreign but violent. Could it be that local violence is not good enough for TV?"

44

Ofit (Colombia)

ABUELITO, SI LOS RICOS VIVEN DE SUS RIQUEZAS, DE QUE VIVIRAN LOS POBRES CUANDO ERRADIQUEN LA POBREZA ABSOLUTA?

—Abuelito, si los ricos viven de sus riquezas, de que vivirán los pobres cuando erradiquen la pobreza absoluta?!

Key Words

abuelito (*n.*, *m.*)	grandfather (diminutive)
ricos (*n.*, *m.*)	rich people
viven (*v.*, vivir *inf.*)	live
riquezas (*n.*, *f.*)	wealth, riches
pobres (*n.*, *m.*)	poor people
cuando (*adv.*)	when
erradiquen (*v.*, erradicar *inf.*)	eradicate, wipe out
pobreza (*n.*, *f.*)	poverty

Everyday English

"Grandpa, if the rich live off their riches, what will the poor have to live on if they wipe out poverty?"

45

Ofit (Colombia)

—¡¡¡Tal como está la situación entonemos ahora el himno nacional pero en tono grave!!!

Key Words

tal como	such as
entonemos (*v.*, entonar *inf.*)	sing
himno nacional (*n., m.*)	national anthem
tono grave	low (minor) key

Everyday English

"The situation has become so serious that we will now sing the national anthem, but in a minor key."

Ofit (Colombia)

—¿Cómo? ¡¡Y ésta fue la única solución para evitar los golpes bajos?!!

Key Words

¿cómo? (*interr.*)	what?
única (*adj.*)	only
evitar (*v., inf.*)	avoid
golpes bajos	low blows

Everyday English

"What? Is this the only way to keep him from hitting below the belt?"

Key Words

quiero (*v.*, querer *inf.*)   wish, want (do)
más fuerte   louder, stronger
vale   good (*exclam.*)

Everyday English

Groom: "I do."
Bride: "Louder."
Groom: "I DO."
Priest: "Good."

Forges (Spain)

Oculista sordo angustiando a un paciente

—La B.
—No señor.
—¡Dios mío, estoy ciego!

Key Words

Dios mío (*exclam.*)	Good Heavens!
ciego (*adj.*)	blind
oculista (*n., m.*)	optometrist
sordo (*adj.*)	deaf
angustiando (*v.*, angustiar *inf.*)	frightening
paciente (*n., m.*)	patient

Everyday English

Deaf optometrist frightening a patient:
"The letter B."
"No."
"Good Heavens, I'm blind!"

Forges (Spain)

—Buenas; vengo a denunciar que, por la 1.237a vez, me han robado la radio del coche.
—Apúntese en aquella pizarra para el "Guiness de records".
—Chasgracias.

Key Words

comisaría (*n., m.*)	police station
buenas	good day
vengo (*v., venir inf.*)	come
denunciar (*v., inf.*)	to make a complaint
vez (*n., m.*)	time
han robado (*v., robar inf.*)	they have stolen, robbed
coche (*n., m.*)	car
apúntese (*v., apuntar inf.*)	include yourself
aquella pizarra	that blackboard
chasgracias	thanks a lot (abbreviation)

Everyday English

"Good day. I've come to complain that the radio in my car has been stolen for the 1,237th time."
"Include yourself on the blackboard over there for the 'Guinness Book of Records.'"
"Thanks a lot."

Forges (Spain)

—Perdone ¿es usted el último?

Key Words

perdone (*v.*, perdonar *inf.*)   excuse me
último (*n.*, *m.*)   last (one)

Everyday English

"Excuse me, are you the last patient?"

—¿Y Manolo?
—En reanimación.

Key Words

Manolo	Manuel (nickname)
reanimación (n., f.)	recovery room

Everyday English

Visitor: "Where's Manolo?"
Mother of quintuplets: "In the recovery room."

—Ahora yo voy a rodearle la cintura con la cinta del vibrador; si tardo uno días en volver no se alarme. Gran viaje.

Key Words

rodearle (*v., inf.*)	go around (you)
cintura (*n., f.*)	waist
cinta del vibrador (*n., f.*)	vibrator belt
tardo (*v.,* tardar *inf.*)	take (time)
unos días	several days
volver (*v., inf.*)	to get back
gran viaje	it's a long trip

Everyday English

"I'm going to put this vibrator belt around your waist. Don't be alarmed if I'm not back in a couple of days. It's a long trip."

Osses (Chile)

—¿Usted me cree tonto? Ahora me dice que va corriendo a la maternidad, y la semana pasada me dijo que iba corriendo a casarse . . .

Key Words

cree (*v.*, creer *inf.*)	think, believe
tonto (*adj.*)	stupid
dice (*v.*, decir *inf.*)	say
corriendo (*v.*, correr *inf.*)	running, rushing
semana pasada	last week
casarse (*v.*, *inf.*)	to get married

Everyday English

"How dumb do you think I am? Now you tell me you're rushing her to the hospital to have a baby, and last week you said you were rushing to get married."

Osses (Chile)

—¡Pero mujer . . . ! En algo debemos pasar el tiempo mientras vienen a socorrernos, ¿no?

Key Words

mujer (*n., f.*)	woman
debemos (*v.,* deber *inf.*)	have to
pasar el tiempo	pass the time
mientras (*conj.*)	while
socorrernos (*v.,* socorrer *inf.*)	to rescue us

Everyday English

"But woman! Don't we need something to do until they come to rescue us?"

—Ya te pedí disculpas. ¿Qué más quieres que te diga?

Key Words

pedí (*v.*, pedir *inf.*)	asked
disculpas (*n.*, *f.*)	forgiveness
quieres (*v.*, querer *inf.*)	want
diga (*v.*, decir *inf.*)	say

Everyday English

"I already said I was sorry. What else do you want me to say?"

Osses (Chile)

—¿Estás bien seguro de que es agua la que vaciaste en el bebedero?

Key Words

seguro (*adj.*)	sure
agua (*n., f.*)	water
vaciaste (*v.,* vaciar *inf.*)	poured
bebedero (*n., m.*)	trough

Everyday English

"Are you sure it was water you put in the trough?"

—No te imaginas la vergonzosa que se ha puesto "La Flor".

Key Words

imaginas (*v.,* imaginar *inf.*)	imagine
vergonzosa (*adj.*)	shy
se ha puesto (*v.,* ponerse *inf.*)	has become
"La Flor"	Flower (name)

Everyday English

"You can't imagine how shy 'La Flor' has become."

Osses (Chile)

—Señor policía, usted se va a reír, pero fue por no atropellar un pollo.

Key Words

reírse (*v., inf.*)   laugh
atropellar (*v., inf.*)   run over
pollo (*n., m.*)   chicken

Everyday English

"Officer, you'll laugh, but I was trying to avoid running over a chicken."

Osses (Chile)

—¿Quieren un lugar para pic-nic? ¡Aquí tienen el mismo lugar donde ustedes pasaron el año pasado!

Key Words

quieren (*v.*, querer *inf.*)	want
lugar (*n., m.*)	place
mismo (*adj.*)	same
pasaron (*v.*, pasar *inf.*)	went through, used
año pasado	last year

Everyday English

"You want a place for a picnic? Here's the spot you had last year."

Osses (Chile)

—¿Su primera guagua? ¿Verdad?

Key Words

primera (*adj.*)	first
guagua (*n., f.*)	baby (Bolivia, Chile)
¿verdad?	right?

Everyday English

"Your first baby, right?"

Osses (Chile)

—No me discuta. ¡Hic! El mejor amigo del hombre es el perro. ¡Hic!

Key Words

discuta (*v.*, discutir *inf.*)	argue
mejor (*adj.*)	best
amigo (*n., m.*)	friend
hombre (*n., m.*)	man
perro (*n., m.*)	dog

Everyday English

"Don't argue with me. Dog is man's best friend!"

Pablo (Spain)

—¡Qué juventud tan contestataria! ¿Por qué no andan como todo el mundo?

Key Words

juventud (*n., f.*)	youth
contestataria (*adj.*)	rebellious
andan (*v.*, andar *inf.*)	walk
todo el mundo	everybody (else)

Everyday English

"Kids have to be different! Why don't they walk like everybody else?"

Pablo (Spain)

—Me estoy poniendo enfermo . . .
—¡Si es que hoy día todos los alimentos están adulterados!

Key Words

poniendo (*v.*, ponerse *inf.*)	turning, becoming
enfermo (*adj.*)	sick
hoy día	nowadays
todos (*adj.*)	all
alimentos (*n., m.*)	foods
adulterados (*adj.*)	adulterated

Everyday English

"I'm getting sick."
"It's today's foods. They're all adulterated."

Pablo (Spain)

—Ya llega la estrella del equipo, que tanto dinero costó al club . . .

Key Words

llega (*v.*, llegar *inf.*)	comes
estrella (*n.*, *f.*)	star
equipo (*n.*, *m.*)	team
dinero (*n.*, *m.*)	money
costó (*v.*, costar *inf.*)	cost

Everyday English

"Here comes the star of the team, the one who cost the club so much money."

Pablo (Spain)

—¡Está dirigiendo "El vals de las olas" de violencia . . . !

Key Words

dirigiendo (*v.*, dirigir *inf.*)	conducting
vals (*n., m.*)	waltz
olas (*n., f.*)	waves

Everyday English

"He's directing the "Waltz of the Waves" as the "Waltz of the Waves of Violence.""

Pablo (Spain)

—Me parece una bobada que bailéis la danza de la lluvia, habiendo nubes de desarrollo horizontal y no soplando vientos del primer cuadrante . . .

Key Words

parece (*v.*, parecer *inf.*)	seems
bobada (*n.*, *f.*)	foolishness
bailéis (*v.*, bailar *inf.*)	dance
danza (*n.*, *f.*)	dance
lluvia (*n.*, *f.*)	rain
habiendo (*v.*, haber *inf.*)	there being
nubes (*n.*, *f.*)	clouds
desarrollo (*n.*, *m.*)	development
soplando (*v.*, soplar *inf.*)	blowing
vientos (*n.*, *m.*)	winds
primer (*adj.*)	primary
cuadrante (*n.*, *m.*)	quadrant

Everyday English

"It seems foolish to me to perform the rain dance when there is a horizontal development of clouds and no winds blowing from the primary quadrant."

Pablo (Spain)

—¡No comprendo qué ve de romántico la gente en la caída de la hoja!

Key Words

comprendo (*v.*, comprender *inf.*)	understand
gente (*n., f.*)	people
caída (*n., f.*)	fall
hoja (*n., f.*)	leaf

Everyday English

"I can't understand why people consider falling leaves so romantic!"

Sayán (Peru)

Key Words

niño (n., m.)	youngster
puedo (v., poder inf.)	can, may
hablar (v., inf.)	speak
dueño (n., m.)	owner
tío (n., m.)	uncle
corral (n., m.)	barn
dándoles (v., dar inf.)	giving them
chanchos (n., m.)	pigs
reconocerá (v., reconocer inf.)	will recognize
único	only one
usa (v., usar inf.)	wearing

Everyday English

"Young man, can I speak with the owner?"

"Yes, ma'am, he's my uncle. He's in the barn feeding the pigs. You'll recognize him because he's the only one wearing a hat."

Sayán (Peru)

—Mami, ¿por qué no mandas a papá temprano a la cama para que yo pueda jugar solito con mi tren?

Key Words

mandas (*v.*, mandar *inf.*)	send
temprano (*adv.*)	early
cama (*n., f.*)	bed
pueda (*v.*, poder *inf.*)	can
jugar (*v., inf.*)	play
solito (*adj.*)	alone
tren (*n., m.*)	train

Everyday English

"Mommy, why don't you send Daddy to bed early so I can play with my train by myself?"

70

Sayán (Peru)

—. . . Qué día, primero me despidieron, luego me multaron por ir con mucha velocidad . . . Sólo me faltaría que tu mamá nos venga a visitar.

Key Words

día (*n., m.*)	day
despidieron (*v., despedir inf.*)	fired
multaron (*v., multar inf.*)	fined
mucha velocidad	too fast
sólo (*adv.*)	only
faltaría (*v., faltar inf.*)	would need
venga (*v., venir inf.*)	come

Everyday English

"What a day! First I was fired, then I was fined for speeding. The only thing I need now is for your mother to come and visit."

Sayán (Peru)

—Efectivamente, señor Saldaña. Todas las personas cometemos errores, pero usted cometió el mismo error el viernes 24 de noviembre de 1982 a las 3 de la tarde.

Key Words

efectivamente (*adv.*)	indeed
cometemos (*v.*, cometer *inf.*)	make
mismo (*adj.*)	same
viernes (*n., m.*)	Friday
las 3 de la tarde	three o'clock in the afternoon

Everyday English

"Indeed, Mr. Saldaña, we all make mistakes. But you made the same mistake on Friday, November 24, 1982, at three in the afternoon."

Sayán (Peru)

—Mejor me salgo, no soporto ver a la gente que trabaja como burro.

Key Words

mejor (*adv.*)	better, best
salgo (*v.*, salir *inf.*)	leave
soporto (*v.*, soportar *inf.*)	tolerate, stand
ver (*v.*, *inf.*)	to see
gente (*n.*, *f.*)	people
trabaja (*v.*, trabajar *inf.*)	work
burro (*n.*, *m.*)	donkey

Everyday English

"I'd better leave. I can't stand to see people working like dogs."

Oki (Costa Rica)

Key Words

infame (*adj.*)	vile
canalla (*n.*, *m.*)	scoundrel
insensible (*adj.*)	insensitive
soporto (*v.*, soportar *inf.*)	endure
vivir (*v.*, *inf.*)	live
contigo	with you
pertenecemos (*v.*, pertenecer *inf.*)	we belong
mundos (*n.*, *m.*)	worlds

Everyday English

"You're a no-good, insensitive scoundrel. I can't bear living with you another minute."

"I'm leaving . . . you and I belong in different worlds."

74

Oki (Costa Rica)

—Y con este nuevo decreto declaro abolida la ley de gravedad.

Key Words

nuevo (*adj.*)	new
decreto (*n., m.*)	decree
declaro (*v.,* declarar *inf.*)	declare
abolida (*v.,* abolir *inf.*)	abolished
ley (*n., f.*)	law
gravedad (*n., f.*)	gravity

Everyday English

"And with this new decree I declare the law of gravity abolished."

Oki (Costa Rica)

—¡No eres más que un pobre cuadrúpedo irracional . . . Yo en cambio, soy todo un bípedo evolucionado!

Key Words

pobre (*adj.*)	poor
irracional (*adj.*)	irrational
cuadrúpedo (*n., m.*)	quadruped (four-footed)
bípedo (*n., m.*)	biped
en cambio	on the other hand

Everyday English

"You are nothing but a poor irrational quadruped . . . I, on the other hand, am a fully evolved biped."

Ruizte (Mexico)

—¡En enero habrá cien medicamentos baratos!
—Me hubiera esperado para enfermarme.

Key Words

enero (*n., m.*)	January
cien (*adj.*)	hundred
medicamentos (*n., m.*)	medicines
baratos (*adj.*)	cheap
hubiera (*v.,* haber *inf.*)	should have
esperado (*v.,* esperar *inf.*)	waited
enfermarme (*v., inf.*)	(for me) to get sick

Everyday English

"In January they're lowering the price on 100 medicines!"
"I should have waited to get sick."

Ruizte (Mexico)

—Ni diga que tiene cucaracha porque le cobran más caro el platillo.

Key Words

diga (*v.*, decir *inf.*)	say
cucaracha (*n.*, *f.*)	cockroach
cobran (*v.*, cobrar *inf.*)	charge
caro (*adj.*)	expensive
platillo (*n.*, *m.*)	dish

Everyday English

"Don't tell them you got a cockroach because they'll charge you more for the dish."

Ruizte (Mexico)

—Ahorita le doy el precio, nomás déjame preguntar cómo amaneció el Dow Jones.

Key Words

ahorita (*adv.*)	right away (Mexico)
doy (*v.,* dar *inf.*)	find out
precio (*n., m.*)	price
nomás (*adv.*)	just (Mexico)
déjeme (*v.,* dejar *inf.*)	let me
preguntar (*v., inf.*)	find out, ask
amaneció (*v.,* amanecer *inf.*)	started the day

Everyday English

"I'll tell you the price right away, as soon as I find out how the Dow Jones opened today."

—Señor, llegó el experto en bolsa.

Key Words

llegó (*v.*, llegar *inf.*)	arrived
bolsa (*n.*, *f.*)	bag; stock market

Everyday English

"Sir, the expert from the market has arrived."

Ruizte (Mexico)

—El niño quedó muy impresionado con el mural de 6 mil metros.

Key Words

niño (*n.*, *m.*)   youngster, boy

quedó (*v.*, quedar *inf.*) turned out to be

Everyday English

"The boy was really impressed with the six-thousand-meter-long mural."

Ruizte (Mexico)

—¿Cuánto por el ramo? ¿A poco lo pintó Van Gogh?

Key Words

¿cuánto? (*interr.*)   how much?

ramo (*n., m.*)   bouquet

a poco (*adv.*)   after all

pintó (*v.,* pintar *inf.*)   painted

Everyday English

"How much for the bouquet? After all, did Van Gogh paint it?"

Ruizte (Mexico)

—¿Murió por plomo? ¿Contaminación?
—No, seis balazos.

Key Words

murió (*v.*, morir *inf.*)	died
plomo (*n., m.*)	lead (metal)
seis (*adj.*)	six
balazos (*n., m.*)	gun shots

Everyday English

"He died from lead poisoning? From something contaminated?"

"No, from six bullets."

Ruizte (Mexico)

—Se va a otorgar el premio nacional de economía.
—Me inscribiste, supongo.

Key Words

otorgar (*v., inf.*)	grant
premio (*n., m.*)	prize
economía (*n., f.*)	economy
inscribiste (*v.,* inscribir *inf.*)	enrolled
supongo (*v.,* suponer *inf.*)	suppose

Everyday English

"They're going to award the national prize for economy."
"You entered my name I suppose."

Ruizte (Mexico)

—No me afectó el aumento a los estacionamientos.

Key Words

aumento (*n.*, *m.*)   increase
estacionamientos (*n.*, *m.*)   parking; parking fees

Everyday English

"The increase in the parking fees didn't affect me."

Ruizte (Mexico)

—Al 08 se reportan los autos robados.
—¿Con todo y una hija?

Key Words

reportan (*v.*, reportar *inf.*)	report
robados (*adj.*)	stolen
hija (*n., f.*)	daughter

Everyday English

"You dial 08 to report a stolen car."
"And an eloped daughter?"

Ruizte (Mexico)

—¡Viejo, ya solucioné nuestro abasto de leche!

Key Words

viejo (*n., m.*)	old man, my dear
solucioné (*v.*, solucionar *inf.*)	solved
abasto (*n., m.*)	supply
leche (*n., f.*)	milk

Everyday English

"Dear, I've solved the problem of our milk supply!"

Ruizte (Mexico)

—¿Por qué es tan prolífica su obra literaria?
—Escribo durante los embotellamientos de tránsito.

Key Words

prolífica (*adj.*)	prolific
obra literaria	literary work
escribo (*v.*, escribir *inf.*)	write
durante (*adv.*)	during
embotellamientos de tránsito (*n., m.*)	traffic jams

Everyday English

"How are you able to produce so many books?"
"I write during traffic jams."

Ruizte (Mexico)

—Los ganadores del Nobel de Medicina descubrieron cómo hacer crecer la piel.

—¿Con todo y el armazón?

Key Words

ganadores (*n., m.*)	winners
descubrieron (*v.,* descubrir *inf.*)	discovered
crecer (*v., inf.*)	grow
piel (*n., f.*)	skin
armazón (*n., f.*)	skeleton

Everyday English

"The winners of the Nobel Prize for Medicine have discovered how to grow skin."

"Can they grow everything else, including the skeleton?"

—Un torero se bordó un logotipo en su traje para vender publicidad.
—¿Y eso es malo?

Key Words

torero (*n., m.*)	bullfighter
bordó (*v.,* bordar *inf.*)	embroidered
logotipo (*n., m.*)	trademark, logo
traje (*n., m.*)	suit
vender (*v., inf.*)	sell
publicidad (*n., f.*)	publicity, advertising
malo (*adj.*)	bad

Everyday English

"A bullfighter embroidered his suit with trademarks to sell advertising."
"And that's bad?"

Ruizte (Mexico)

—Sí, efectivamente voy a hacer un retiro.

Key Words

efectivamente (*adv.*)   as a matter of fact
retiro (*n., m.*)   withdrawal

Everyday English

"Yes, as a matter of fact, I've come to make a withdrawal."

Ruizte (Mexico)

—¿Está anegada la calle, mi amor?

Key Words

anegada (*v.*, anegar *inf.*)	flooded
calle (*n.*, *f.*)	street
mi amor	my love

Everyday English

"Is the street flooded, dear?"

Ruizte (Mexico)

—Esto significa que no tienes dinero para irnos de vacaciones.

Key Words

esto (*pron.*)	this
significa (*v.*, significar *inf.*)	means, signifies
dinero (*n., m.*)	money
vacaciones (*n., f., pl.*)	vacation

Everyday English

"This means you don't have the money to take us on a vacation."

Elcíades (Colombia)

—¡No te preocupes por compañía, él me dijo que me esperaba acompañado de su mejor amigo!

Key Words

preocupes (*v.*, preocupar *inf.*)	worry
compañía (*n.*, *f.*)	company
dijo (*v.*, decir *inf.*)	told, said
esperaba (*v.*, esperar *inf.*)	waiting for, expecting
acompañado (*v.*, acompañar *inf.*)	accompanied
mejor	best
amigo (*n.*, *m.*)	friend

Everyday English

"Don't worry about having an escort; he told me he'd be waiting for me with his best friend."

Elcíades (Colombia)

—Por favor saque la lengua.
—Pero si lo que me duele es el estómago.
—Bueno . . . saque el estómago.

Key Words

saque (*v.*, sacar *inf.*)	stick out
lengua (*n.*, *f.*)	tongue
duele (*v.*, doler *inf.*)	hurts
estómago (*n.*, *m.*)	stomach

Everyday English

Doctor: "Stick out your tongue."
Patient: "But it's my stomach that hurts."
Doctor: "O.K. Stick out your stomach."

Elcíades (Colombia)

—Comenzando ganará $30 mil al mes, después $100 mil . . .
—Está bien . . . ¡entonces vengo después!

Key Words

comenzando (*v.*, comenzar *inf.*)	starting
ganará (*v.*, ganar *inf.*)	will earn
al mes	per month
después (*adv.*)	later
entonces (*adv.*)	then

Everyday English

"You'll start at 30,000 a month, later you'll get 100,000 . . ."
"Good . . . then I'll come back later!"

Elcíades (Colombia)

—Por favor, no me ponga "esposas" que quiero seguir siendo "soltero".

Key Words

ponga (*v.*, poner *inf.*)	put, place
esposas (*n.*, *f.*)	handcuffs
	singular: wife
quiero (*v.*, querer *inf.*)	want
seguir (*v.*, *inf.*)	continue
siendo (*v.*, ser *inf.*)	being
soltero (*adj.*)	unmarried

Everyday English

"Please don't handcuff me, I don't want to be tied down."

Elcíades (Colombia)

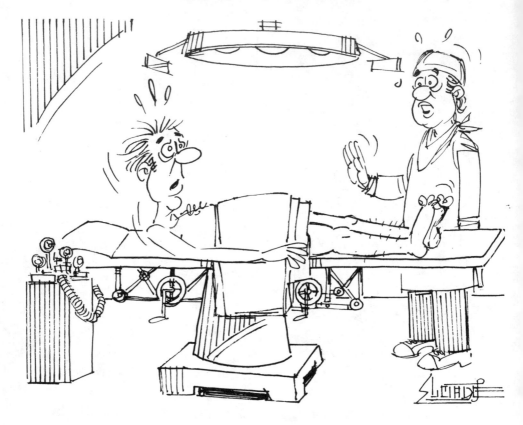

—Tengo miedo doctor, es la "primera" vez que me operan . . .
—Tranquilo . . . ¡También ésta es mi "primera" operación!

Key Words

tengo miedo (*v.*, tener miedo *inf.*)	I'm afraid
primera vez	first time
operan (*v.*, operar *inf.*)	operate on

Everyday English

Patient: "I'm frightened doctor, this is the first time I've been operated on."
Doctor: "Relax . . . it's also my first operation."

Elcíades (Colombia)

—Ahora . . . para aquél que he considerado siempre como mi "amigo fiel" . . .

Key Words

aquél (*pron.*)	the one
considerado (*v.*, considerar *inf.*)	considered
siempre (*adv.*)	always
amigo (*n., m.*)	friend
fiel (*adj.*)	faithful

Everyday English

"Now . . . for the one I've always considered my faithful friend . . ."

—¿Perdió algo, señor . . . ?
—¡Sí . . . el "equilibrio" . . . !

Key Words

| perdió (*v.*, perder *inf.*) | lost |
| algo (*pron.*) | something |

Everyday English

"Did you lose something sir?"
"Yes—my balance!"

Elcíades (Colombia)

—¿Saben por qué no sale el sol de noche? . . . ¡porque se quebrarían las empresas de alumbrado!

Key Words

saben (*v.*, saber *inf.*)	know
sale (*v.*, salir *inf.*)	come out
sol (*n.*, *m.*)	sun
noche (*n.*, *f.*)	night
quebrarían (*v.*, quebrar *inf.*)	would go broke
empresas (*n.*, *f.*)	companies
alumbrado (*n.*, *m.*)	lighting

Everyday English

"Do you know why the sun doesn't come out at night? Because the electric companies would go broke!"

Spanish-English Glossary

Verbs are listed in the infinitive form. Reflexive verbs are followed by *se*. Nouns are listed in singular form unless used in the plural (like *vacaciones, vacation*).

For additional Spanish words, see *Five Important Verbs, The Pronouns,* and *The Little Words.*

In both glossaries, the entries are followed by the pages on which the words can be found.

a poco after all, 82
abasto supply, 87
abolir to abolish, 36, 75
abuelita grandmother, 17
abuelito grandfather, 45
acabar to end, 4
acompañar to accompany, 94
acostarse to go to bed, 35
adulterado adulterated, 64
agua water, 57
ahí there, 38
ahorita right away, 79
al mes per month, 95
alérgico allergic, 37
algo something, 100
algo de malo anything wrong, 43
alguna any, 13
algunos some, 31
alimento food, 64
almohada pillow, 41
almorzar to have lunch, 29
alumbrado lighting, 101
amanecer to start the day, 79
amigo friend, 62, 94, 99
andar to walk, 63
anegar to flood, 92
angustiar to frighten, 49
año pasado last year, 60
apúntese include yourself, 50
aquél that one, 99
aquella pizarra that blackboard, 50
arma weapon, 4

armazón skeleton, 89
asegurar to insure, 25
así es that's it, 5
astronauta astronaut, 37
atropellar to run over, 59
aumento increase, 85
avisar to tell, 24
ayudar to help, 21

bailar to dance, 67
bajar to go down, 29
balazo gunshot, 83
balón ball, 43
barato cheap, 77
bebedero trough, 57
bípedo biped, 76
bobada folly, 67
bola de cristal crystal ball, 10
bolsa bag; stock market, 80
boquita bite (to eat), 9
bordar to embroider, 90
borracho drunk, 2
borrar to erase, 13
buenas good day, 50
bueno good, 44
burro donkey, 73

cacerola frying pan, 6
cada vez que whenever, 17
caída fall, 68
calmar to soothe, 33
calle street, 92
cama bed, 70

embotellamiento de
  tránsito traffic jam, 88
embuste lie, 3
empresa company, 101
en cambio on the other hand,
  76
en caso de in case of, 19
encantador charming, 42
enero January, 77
enfermarse to get sick, 77
enfermedad illness, 19
enfermo sick, 64
entonar to sing, 46
entonces then, 96
entrar to enter, 38
equipo team, 65
erradicar to eradicate, to
  wipe out, 45
esclavitud slavery, 36
escribir to write, 5, 88
especialista specialist, 22
esperar to wait, 77, 94
esposa wife, 97
esposas handcuffs, 97
estacionamiento parking,
  85
esto this, 93
estómago stomach, 95
estrella star, 65
estúpido stupid person, 32
evitar to avoid, 47
extranjero foreign, 44

faltar to need, 71
fiel faithful, 99
final end, 14
financiar to finance, 31
fondos funds, 1
francés French, 15

ganador winner, 89
ganar to earn, 96
garganta throat, 17, 22
gente people, 44, 68, 73

golpes bajos low blows, 47
gran viaje it's a long trip,
  53
gravedad gravity, 74
guagua baby, 61
gustar to like, 40

haber to be, 3, 67, 77
hablar to speak, 25, 32, 69
helado ice cream, 27
heredero heir, 34
hija daughter, 86
hijo son, 6, 16, 30
himno nacional national
  anthem, 46
hoja leaf, 68
hombre man, 4, 36, 62
hoy día nowadays, 64

imaginar to imagine, 58
infame vile, 74
informar to inform, 39
ingresar to enter, 39
inscribir to enroll, 84
insensible insensitive, 74
intentar to try, 30
ir to go, 28
irse to leave, 7
irracional irrational, 76

jamás never, 4
jugar to play, 70
juventud youth, 63

La Flor Flower (*name*), 58
las tres de la tarde three
  o'clock in the afternoon, 72
leche milk, 87
lengua tongue, 95
ley law, 75
libro book, 5
liga league, 26
línea line, 2
loco crazy, 29

poder to be able to, can, 2, 39, 69, 70
pollo chicken, 59
por lo menos at least, 33
poner to put, 97; to wear, 18
ponerse to become, 58, 64
precio price, 79
preguntar to ask, 28; to find out, 79
premio prize, 84
preocupar to worry, 14, 94
primer primary, 67
primera first, 61
primera vez first time, 98
primo cousin, 38
prolífica prolific, 88
prometer to promise, 15
psicología psychology, 30
publicidad advertising, 90

quebrar to go broke, 101
quedar to turn out to be, 81
quedarse to stay, 28
queja complaint, 33
quejarse to complain, 44
querer to want, 48, 58, 60, 97
querido dear, 6

ramo bouquet, 82
raza humana human race, 4
reanimación recovery room, 52
recién recently, 39
reconocer to recognize, 69
recta straight, 2
reglamentario pertaining to regulations, 42
reírse to laugh, 59
repartir to share, 34
reportar to report, 86
retiro withdrawal, 91
ricos rich people, 45
rincón corner, 17
riqueza wealth, 45

robado stolen, 86
robar to steal, 50
rodear to go around, 53
romper to break, 19
rubia blonde, 21

saber to know, 101
sacar to stick out, 95
salir to come out, 38, 101; to leave, 38, 73
seguir to follow, 2; to continue, 97
segundo piso second floor, 3
seguro sure, 57
seis six, 83
semana pasada last week, 54
ser to be, 28, 97
siempre always, 99
significar to mean, 93
sistema system, 33
socorrer to rescue, 55
sol sun, 101
solito alone, 70
sólo only, 34, 71
soltero unmarried, 97
solucionar to solve, 33, 87
soplar to blow, 67
soportar to tolerate, 73, 74
sordo deaf, 49
sugerencia suggestion, 33
suponer to suppose, 84

tal como such as, 46
tal vez perhaps, 42
tardar to take (time), 53
teledirigido radio-controlled, 43
temor fear, 35
temprano early, 70
tener to have, 13
tener miedo to be afraid, 98
terremoto earthquake, 35
tío uncle, 69
tirar to throw away, 17

todavía still, 1
todo all, 64
todo el mundo everybody
  (else), 63
tono grave minor key, 46
tonto stupid, 54
torero bullfighter, 90
trabajar to work, 73
traer to bring, 9
traje suit, 90
tránsito traffic, 29, 88
tras de ser besides being, 44
tren train, 70
tres three, 27

último last, 51
único only, only one, 47, 69
unos días several days, 53
usar to use, 10, 30; to wear,
  69
utilizar to use, 4

vacaciones vacation, 93
vaciar to pour, 57

vale (*exclam.*) good, 48
vals waltz, 66
vecina neighbor, 3
vejez old age, 14
vender to sell, 90
venenoso poisonous, 11
venir to come, 40, 50, 71
ver to see, 17, 29, 38, 73; to
  watch, 3
verdad (*exclam.*) right, 61
verdad, de truly, 11
vergonzosa shy, 58
vestir to dress, 35
vez time, 17, 50
vida life, 14
vidrio glass, 19
viejo old man, 87
viento wind, 67
viernes Friday, 72
vivir to live, 16, 45, 74
volver to return, to get back,
  53
volver a to do again, 15

English-Spanish Glossary

abolish abolir, 38, 74
accompany acompañar, 94
adulterated adulterado, 64
advertisement el consejo comercial, 31
advertising la publicidad, 90
afraid, to be tener miedo, 98
after all a poco, 82
all todo, 64
allergic alérgico, 37
alone solito, 70
always siempre, 99
any alguna, 13
anything wrong algo de malo, 43
argue discutir, 62
arrive llegar, 80
as a matter of fact efectivamente, 72, 91
ask preguntar, 28, 79
ask (for) pedir, 56
astronaut el astronauta, 37
at least por lo menos, 33
avoid evitar, 47

baby la guagua, 61
bad malo, 90
bag la bolsa, 80
ball el balón, 43
barn el corral, 69
be ser, 26, 97; haber, 3, 67, 77
be able poder, 2, 39
become ponerse, 58, 64
bed la cama, 70
bed (to go to) acostarse, 35
beer la cerveza, 27
believe creer, 20, 35, 54
besides being tras de ser, 44
best mejor, 62, 73, 94

biped el bípedo, 76
bite (to eat) la boquita, 9
blackboard, that aquella pizarra, 50
blind ciego, 49
blonde la rubia, 21
blow soplar, 67
book el libro, 5
bouquet el ramo, 82
boy el niño, 69, 81
break romper, 19
bring traer, 9
brunette la morena, 21
bullfighter el torero, 90

can (v.) poder, 2, 39, 69, 71
car el coche, 50
chance la casualidad, 20
charge cobrar, 78
charming encantador, 42
cheap barato, 77
checkbook la chequera, 1
chicken el pollo, 59
cloud la nube, 67
cockroach la cucaracha, 78
coincidence la casualidad, 20
come venir, 40, 50, 71; llegar, 65
come out salir, 38, 101
company la compañía, 94; la empresa, 101
complain quejarse, 44
complaint la queja, 33
conduct (v.) dirigir, 66
consider considerar, 99
continue seguir, 97
corner el rincón, 17
cost (v.) costar, 65
cousin el primo, 38
crazy loco, 29; peligroso, 29
cream la crema, 13
crystal ball la bola de cristal, 10

dance (v.) bailar, 67
dance la danza, 67
dangerous peligroso, 29
daughter la hija, 86
day el día, 71
deaf sordo, 49
dear querido, 6
debt la deuda, 34
decide decidir, 21
declare declarar, 75
decree el decreto, 75
deny negar, 42
development el desarrollo, 67
die morir, 83
difficult difícil, 33
direct (v.) dirigir, 66
discover descubrir, 89
dish (of food) el platillo, 78
do again volver a, 15
dog el perro, 62
donkey el burro, 73
dress (v.) vestir, 35
drunk borracho, 2
during durante, 88

ear el oído, 22
early temprano, 70
earn ganar, 96
earthquake el terremoto, 35
economy la economía, 84
embroider bordar, 90
end (v.) acabar, 4
end el final, 14
endure soportar, 74
enroll inscribir, 84
enter entrar, 38
enter (as member) ingresar, 39
eradicate erradicar, 45
erase borrar, 14
everybody (else) todo el mundo, 63
excuse me disculpe, 40; perdone, 51

expensive caro, 78
expensive, very carísimo, 31
eye el ojo, 3

faithful fiel, 99
fall la caída, 68
fast (too) mucha velocidad, 71
fear el temor, 35
fiction de cuentos, 20
fight la pelea, 3
finance financiar, 31
find out dar, 79; preguntar, 79
fine (v.) multar, 71
fire (v.) despedir, 24, 71
first primera, 61
first time primera vez, 98
flood (v.) anegar, 92
Flower La Flor (name), 58
follow seguir, 2
food el alimento, 64
foolishness la bobada, 67
foreign extranjero, 44
forget olvidar, 5
forgiveness disculpas, 56
frame el marco, 42
French francés, 16
Friday viernes, 72
friend el amigo, 62, 94, 99
frighten angustiar, 49
frying pan la cacerola, 6
funds los fondos, 1

get back volver, 53
give dar, 69
glass el vidrio, 19
go ir, 28
go around rodear, 53
go broke quebrarse, 101
go down bajar, 29
go through pasar, 60
goal el marco, 42
good bueno, 44

good (*exclam.*) vale, 48
good day buenas, 50
good heavens Dios mío, 49
grandfather el abuelito, 45
grandmother la abuelita, 17
grant (*v.*) otorgar, 84
gravity la gravedad, 75
grow crecer, 89
gunshot el balazo, 83

handcuffs las esposas, 97
have tener, 13
have to deber, 34, 55
heaven el cielo, 14
heir el heredero, 34
help (*v.*) ayudar, 21
how much? ¿cuánto? 82
human race la raza humana, 14
hundred cien, 77
hurt doler, 95
husband el marido, 3, 37

ice cream el helado, 27
illness la enfermedad, 19
imagine imaginar, 58
in case of en caso de, 19
include yourself apúntese, 50
increase el aumento, 85
indeed efectivamente, 72, 91
inform informar, 39
inhabitant (of a capital) capitalino, 16
insensitive insensible, 74
insure asegurar, 26
irrational irracional, 76
it's a long trip gran viaje, 53

January enero, 77
just nomás, 79

knot el nudo, 17
know saber, 101

last último, 51
last week la semana pasada, 54
last year el año pasado, 60
later después, 96
laugh reírse, 59
law la ley, 75
lead el plomo, 83
leaf la hoja, 68
league la liga, 26
leave dejar, 34; irse, 7; salir, 38, 73
let dejar, 79
let's hope ojalá, 4
lie el embuste, 3
life la vida, 14
lighting el alumbrado, 101
like (*v.*) gustar, 40
line la línea, 2
literary work la obra literaria, 88
little dove la palomita, 8
live (*v.*) vivir, 16, 45, 74
local criolla, 44
long time mucho tiempo, 28
look mirar, 36
lose perder, 100
louder más fuerte, 48
low blows los golpes bajos, 47
lunch (*v.*) almorzar, 29

make cometer, 72
make a complaint denunciar, 50
man el hombre, 4, 36, 62
Manuel Manolo (*nickname*), 52
marriage counselor el consejero matrimonial, 32
marry casarse, 54

mean (v.)   significar, 93
medicine   el medicamento, 77
memoirs   las memorias, 5
milk   la leche, 87
minor key   el tono grave, 46
money   el dinero, 14, 65, 93
month, per   al mes, 96
my love   mi amor, 8, 15, 18, 92

national anthem   el himno
   nacional, 46
need   faltar, 71
neighbor   la vecina, 3
nerves   los nervios, 33
never   jamás, 4; nunca, 15
new   nuevo, 75
news   las noticias, 6
night   la noche, 101
nobody   nadie, 18
nose   la nariz, 22
notice   notar, 18
nowadays   hoy día, 64

office   la oficina, 18, 39, 40
old age   la vejez, 14
old man   el viejo, 87
on the other hand   en
   cambio, 76
one, the   aquél, 99
only (adv.)   sólo, 34, 71
only, only one   único, 47, 70
operate on   operar, 98
optometrist   el oculista, 49
order (v.)   ordenar, 15
other   otro, 5
oust   echar, 7
owner   el dueño, 69

paint (v.)   pintar, 21, 82
parking   el estacionamiento,
   85
pass the time   pasar el
   tiempo, 56
patient   el paciente, 49

peace   la paz, 25
people   la gente, 44, 68, 73
perhaps   tal vez, 42
pig   el cerdo, 8; el chancho, 69
pillow   la almohada, 41
place   el lugar, 60
plan   el plan, 25
play (v.)   jugar, 70
poisonous   venenoso, 11
police station   la comisaría,
   50
poor   pobre, 23, 76
poor (people)   los pobres, 45
pork rind   chicharrón, 9
pour   vaciar, 57
poverty   la pobreza, 45
price   el precio, 79
primary   primer, 67
prize   el premio, 84
prolific   prolífica, 88
promise (v.)   prometer, 15
psychology   la psicología, 30
put   poner, 97
put on   ponerse, 18

quadrant   el cuadrante, 67
quadruped   el cuadrúpedo, 76
quarrel (v.)   pelear, 34

radio-controlled   teledirigido,
   43
rain (v.)   llover, 14
rain   la lluvia, 67
really   de verdad, 11
rebellious   contestataria, 63
recently   recién, 39
recognize   reconocer, 69
recovery room   la
   reanimación, 52
**regulations, pertaining
   to**   reglamentario, 42
report (v.)   reportar, 86
request   la petición, 33
rescue   socorrer, 55

return volver, 53
rich people los ricos, 45
right (exclam.) verdad, 61
right away ahorita, 79
run correr, 54
run over atropellar, 59

same misma, mismo, 8, 23,
    60, 72
say decir, 7, 10, 54, 56, 78, 94
scoundrel canalla, 74
second floor el segundo piso,
    3
see ver, 18, 29, 38, 73
seem parecer, 67
sell vender, 90
send mandar, 70
several days unos días, 53
share repartir, 34
shy vergonzosa, 58
sick enfermo, 64
sick, to get enfermarse, 77
sing entonar, 47
six seis, 83
skeleton el armazón, 89
skin la piel, 89
slavery la esclavitud, 36
solve solucionar, 33, 87
some algunos, 31
something algo, 100
son el hijo, 6, 16, 30
soothe calmar, 33
speak hablar, 25, 32, 69
specialist el especialista, 22
spot la mancha, 13
star la estrella, 65
start comenzar, 96
start the day amanecer, 79
stay quedarse, 28
steal robar, 52
stick out sacar, 95
still todavía, 1
stock market la bolsa, 80
stolen robado, 86

stomach el estómago, 95
stories los cuentos, 20
straight recta, 2
street la calle, 92
stupid tonto, 54
stupid person el estúpido, 32
such as tal como, 46
suffer padecer, 23
suggestion la sugerencia, 33
suit el traje, 90
sun el sol, 101
supply el abasto, 87
suppose suponer, 84
sure seguro, 57
system el sistema, 33

take (time) tardar, 53
talk hablar, 32
team el equipo, 66
tell avisar, 24
thanks a lot chasgracias, 50
that's it así es, 5
then entonces, 96
there ahí, 38
thing la cosa, 20
think pensar, 8, 12; creer, 54
this esto, 93
three tres, 27
**three o'clock in the
    afternoon** las tres de la
    tarde, 72
throat la garganta, 17, 22
throw away tirar, 17
time la vez, 50
tolerate soportar, 73, 74
tongue la lengua, 95
too fast mucha velocidad, 71
toupee el peluquín, 18
trademark el logotipo, 90
traffic el tránsito, 29
traffic jam el embotella-
    miento de tránsito, 88
train el tren, 70
trough el bebedero, 58

English-Spanish Subject Index

Positive and Negative Thoughts and Feelings

Actions

give dar, 69
imagine imaginar, 58
look mirar, 36
order (v.) ordenar, 15
pass the time pasar el
  tiempo, 55
put poner, 97
put on ponerse, 18
recognize reconocer, 69
say decir, 7, 10, 54, 56, 78, 94
see ver, 17, 29, 38, 73

seem parecer, 67
speak hablar, 25, 32, 69
start comenzar, 96
stick out sacar, 95
suppose suponer, 84
talk hablar, 32
tell avisar, 24
throw away tirar, 17
use usar, 10, 30; utilizar, 4
wait esperar, 77, 94
watch ver, 3

When and How Much?

after all a poco, 82
all todo, 64
always siempre, 99
any alguna, 13
as a matter of fact
  efectivamente, 72, 91
at least por lo menos, 33
besides being tras de ser, 44
during durante, 88
early temprano, 70
end (v.) acabar, 4
end el final, 14
fast, too mucha velocidad, 71
first primera, 61
first time primera vez, 98
Friday viernes, 72
how come? ¿cómo? 47
how much? ¿cuánto? 82
hundred cien, 76
in case of en caso de, 19
include yourself apúntese,
  50
indeed efectivamente, 72, 91
January enero, 77
just nomás, 79
last último, 51
last week la semana pasada,
  54
last year el año pasado, 60
later después, 96

long time mucho tiempo, 28
louder más fuerte, 48
month, per al mes, 96
never jamás, 13; nunca, 15
night la noche, 101
nowadays hoy día, 64
on the other hand en
  cambio, 76
one, the aquél, 99
only (adv.) sólo, 34, 71
only, only one único, 47, 69
other otro, 5
perhaps tal vez, 42
prolific prolífica, 88
really de verdad, 10
recently recién, 39
right (exclam.) verdad,
  61
right away ahorita, 79
same misma, mismo, 8, 23,
  60, 72
several days unos días, 53
six seis, 83
some algunos, 31
still todavía, 1
straight recta, 2
such as tal como, 46
that's it así es, 5
then entonces, 96
three tres, 27

Quality of Life

Nature

People among Themselves

flower   La Flor (*name*), 58
foreign   extranjero, 44
French   francés, 15
friend   el amigo, 62, 94, 99
grandfather   el abuelito, 45
grandmother   la abuelita, 17
heir   el heredero, 34
human race   la raza humana, 4
husband   el marido, 3, 37
inhabitant (of a capital)   capitalino, 16
little dove   la palomita, 8
man   el hombre, 4, 36, 62
Manuel   Manolo (*nickname*), 52
marry (v.)   casarse, 54
memoirs   las memorias, 5
my love   mi amor, 8, 15, 18, 92
neighbor   el vecino, 3
nobody   nadie, 18

nose   la nariz, 22
old man   el viejo, 87
parking   el estacionamiento, 85
people   la gente, 44, 68, 73
play (v.)   jugar, 70
son   el hijo, 6, 16, 30
stomach   el estómago, 95
suit   el traje, 90
throat   la garganta, 17, 22
tongue   la lengua, 95
toupee   el peluquín, 18
turn out to be   quedar, 81
uncle   el tío, 69
unmarried   soltero, 97
waist   la cintura, 53
wear   ponerse, 18; usar, 69
wife   la esposa, 97
with you   contigo, 74
woman   la mujer, 26, 55
youngster   el niño, 69, 81

Where and How to Go

arrive   llegar, 80
car   el coche, 50
come   venir, 40, 50, 71; llegar, 65
come out   salir, 38, 101
enter   entrar, 38
get back   volver, 53
go   ir, 28
go around   rodear, 53
go down   bajar, 29
go through   pasar, 60
have a good trip   gran viaje, 53
leave   dejar, 34; irse, 7; salir, 38, 73
let   dejar, 79

place   el lugar, 60
recovery room   la reanimación, 52
return   volver, 53
run   correr, 54
send   mandar, 70
stay   quedarse, 28
street   la calle, 92
take (time)   tardar, 53
there   ahí, 38
traffic   el tránsito, 29
traffic jam   el embotellamiento de tránsito, 88
train   el tren, 70
vacation   las vacaciones, 93
walk   andar, 63

Around the House and Farm

barn   el corral, 69
bed   la cama, 70
bed (to go to)   acostarse, 35
book   el libro, 5
bouquet   el ramo, 82
chicken   el pollo, 59
corner   el rincón, 17
dog   el perro, 62
dress (v.)   vestir, 35
glass   el vidrio, 19

grow   crecer, 89
lighting   el alumbrado, 101
little dove   la palomita, 8
medicine   el medicamento, 77
pig   el cerdo, 8; el chancho, 69
pillow   la almohada, 41
second floor   el segundo piso, 3
trough   el bebedero, 57

Thoughts, Feelings, and Conditions

afraid, to be   tener miedo, 98
allergic   alérgico, 37
anything wrong   algo de malo, 43
be   ser, 26, 97; haber, 3, 67, 77
be able to   poder, 2, 39, 69, 70
become   ponerse, 58, 64
believe   creer, 20, 35, 54
biped   el bípedo, 76
blind   ciego, 49
blonde (n.)   la rubia, 21
brunette (n.)   la morena, 21
can (v.)   poder, 2, 39, 69, 70
charming   encantador, 42
consider   considerar, 99
crazy   loco, 29
dangerous   peligroso, 29
deaf   sordo, 49
difficult   difícil, 34

drunk   borracho, 2
faithful   fiel, 99
fear   el temor, 35
foolishness   la bobada, 67
insensitive   insensible, 74
irrational   irracional, 76
nerves   los nervios, 33
old age   la vejez, 14
poisonous   venenoso, 11
quadruped   el cuadrúpedo, 76
rebellious   contestataria, 63
scoundrel   canalla, 74
shy   vergonzosa, 58
sick   enfermo, 64
sick, to get   enfermarse, 77
stupid   tonto, 54
stupid person   el estúpido, 32
vile   infame, 74
youth   la juventud, 63

Earning a Living

advertisement   el consejo comercial, 31
advertising   la publicidad, 90
astronaut   el astronauta, 37
bullfighter   el torero, 90
charge   cobrar, 78
checkbook   la chequera, 1

company   la compañía, 94; la empresa, 101
conduct (v.)   dirigir, 66
cost (v.)   costar, 65
debt   la deuda, 34
direct (v.)   dirigir, 66
earn   ganar, 96

economy la economía, 84
embroider bordar, 90
fight (n.) la pelea, 3
finance (v.) financiar, 31
goal el marco, 42
funds los fondos, 1
go broke quebrarse, 101
law la ley, 75
league la liga, 26
literary work la obra
literaria, 88
marriage counselor el
consejero matrimonial, 32
money el dinero, 14, 65, 93
office la oficina, 18, 39, 40
operate on operar, 98
optometrist el oculista, 49
owner el dueño, 69
paint (v.) pintar, 21, 82

patient el paciente, 49
plan el plan, 25
police station la comisaría,
50
price el precio, 79
psychology la psicología, 30
**regulations, pertaining
to** reglamentario, 42
report reportar, 86
sell vender, 90
specialist el especialista, 22
star la estrella, 65
stock market la bolsa, 80
suggestion la sugerencia, 33
system el sistema, 33
trademark el logotipo, 90
work (v.) trabajar, 73
write escribir, 5, 88

Food and Drink

beer la cerveza, 27
bite (to eat) la boquita, 9
dish (of food) el platillo, 78
food el alimento, 64
frying pan la cacerola, 6

ice cream el helado, 27
lunch (v.) almorzar, 29
milk la leche, 87
pork rind el chicharrón, 9
pour vaciar, 57

Leisure Time Activities

ball el balón, 43
dance (v.) bailar, 67
dance la danza, 67
sing entonar, 46

team el equipo, 65
waltz el vals, 66
winner el ganador, 89

What Things?